HALF for YOU
HALF for ME

A Story from India

Raj and Han were brothers,
and they liked to share things
whenever they could.

"Half for you
and half for me," they said.

Then one day
Raj became greedy.

He began to cheat Han.

3

"Let's share this goat,"
said Raj.
"You have the front half,
and I'll have the back half."

Every day, Han fed
his half of the goat.
And every day Raj milked
his half of the goat
and sold the milk.

"Hmmm," thought Han.

Then one day
Raj said,
"Let's share
this cornfield.
You have the field
in winter and spring.
I'll have it for
the other half
of the year."

6

In winter, Han watched
as snow covered
his cornfield.

Then in spring
he worked hard,
planting and watering.

In summer, Raj watched *his* corn grow.

Then in autumn he sold it.

"Hmmm," thought Han.

Then came another day,
and Raj said,
"Let's share this pear tree.
You have the bottom half,
and I'll have the top half."

Every day, Han watered
the tree.

Then Raj picked the pears
and sold them.

"Hmmm," thought Han.
"This is not *real* sharing."
And he decided
what to do.

The next day, when Raj
was milking the goat,
Han tickled its nose.
And the goat
kicked the milk over.

"Why did you do that?"
Raj asked Han crossly.

"I can do what I like
with my half of the goat,"
said Han.

"I've got a better idea,"
said Raj. "Let's both
take care of the goat.
And let's share the money
when we sell the milk."

The next day, Han told Raj
that he would not be
working in the cornfield
during spring.

"Why not?" said Raj.

"I can do what I like
when the cornfield is mine,"
said Han.

"I've got a better idea,"
said Raj. "Let's both
work in the field.
And let's share
the money when
we sell the corn."

Han agreed to that.

19

The next day, Han started to chop down the pear tree.

"Stop that!" shouted Raj.

"Why should I?" said Han. "I can do what I like with my half of the pear tree."

"I've got a better idea,"
said Raj. "Let's both
take care of the tree.
And let's share
the money when
we sell the pears."

Han agreed to that.

From that day, Raj and Han
really shared everything —
even the work.

"Half for you
and half for me," they said.